W9-CLX-388

Wackiest Jokes in the World

by
Michael J. Pellowski

illustrated by
Sanford Hoffman

Sterling Publishing Co., Inc., New York

Claymont Schools
Northside L.R.C.

92398   BTSD   11/94 $12.37

Thanks to Judy for helping me smile
through the tough times and to God
for giving me the gift of laughter.

Library of Congress Cataloging-in-Publication Data

Pellowski, Michael.
 Wackiest jokes in the world / Michael J. Pellowski ; illustrated by Sanford
Hoffman.
  p.   cm.
 Includes index.
 ISBN 0-8069-0493-3
 1. Wit and humor, Juvenile. [1. Riddles. 2. Jokes. 3. Knock-knock
jokes.] I. Hoffman, Sanford, ill. II. Title.
PN6163.P446   1994
818'.5402—dc20   93-38242
                                                            CIP
                                                             AC

10 9 8 7 6 5 4 3 2 1

Published by Sterling Publishing Company, Inc.
387 Park Avenue South, New York, N.Y. 10016
© 1994 by Michael J. Pellowski
Distributed in Canada by Sterling Publishing
% Canadian Manda Group, P.O. Box 920, Station U
Toronto, Ontario, Canada M8Z 5P9
Distributed in Great Britain and Europe by Cassell PLC
Villiers House, 41/47 Strand, London WC2N 5JE, England
Distributed in Australia by Capricorn Link (Australia) Pty Ltd.
P.O. Box 6651, Baulkham Hills, Business Centre, NSW 2153, Australia
Manufactured in the United States of America
All rights reserved

Sterling ISBN 0-8069-0493-3

CONTENTS

1. FAMOUS FUNNIES

What owl comes out at night and robs the rich to give to the poor?
Robin Hoot.

What sheep lives in a cave and has a secret identity?
Baaman.

Which cat discovered America?
Christofurry Columbus.

What cow is a famous rock singer?
Moodonna.

What did the baby chicks say when Mr. Scrooge walked by?

"Cheap! Cheap! Cheap!"

What cartoon dog is always covered with moisture in the morning?

Scooby Dew.

What muppet is always covered with dew?

Mist Piggy.

What cartoon show stars a squirrel and an old steer?

Rocky and Bullwrinkled.

Why did Ronald McDonald go to the eye doctor?

He kept seeing double cheeseburgers.

Turtle Power

How do you knock out a turtle superhero?
Hit him on the ninjaw.

What kind of gas do Ninja Turtles use?
Shell.

HAL: How do Ninja Turtles dye their skin?
AL: They use mu-tint.

Which turtle superhero is green and bumpy?
Pickleangelo.

Which turtle superhero is dopey?
Leo-nerdo!

Which turtle superhero hears ringing in his ears?
Don-a-telephone-O!

What did the Ninja Turtles shout when the lady crashed into their van?
"Sewer!"

What would you get if you crossed a cow with a superhero that has a shell?

A moo-tant Ninja Turtle.

MILLIE: What job did little Bruce Wayne have at the baseball stadium?

TILLIE: He was a bat boy.

What do you get when Batman falls off the Empire State Building?

Splatman!

Famous Skunks

Inventor—
Alexander Graham Smell

Which video games use yarn?

Super Knit-tendo.

Who eats spinach and sews suits?

Popeye the Tailor Man.

Who is sticky and has webbed feet?
  Taffy Duck.

What's the name of the stupidest amusement park in the world?
  Ditzyland.

What would you call an exact duplicate of Texas?
  The Clone Star State.

SALLY: What toy grows in your garden?
ALLEY: Cabbage Patch Dolls, of course.

What has leaves and is really silly?
  The Tree Stooges.

What's funny and makes you itch?
  The Flea Stooges.

King of Comedy

What was Elvis's favorite song when he was a baby?
"*Goo Suede Shoes.*"

What did Elvis sing at the animal shelter?
"*You Ain't Nothing But a Pound Dog.*"

What is the favorite song of Elvis's ghost?
"*Boo Suede Shoes.*"

Who is the king of the rock garden?
Elvis Parsley.

RICK: Where does Elvis Purple live?
NICK: In Grapeland.

What's short, lives at the North Pole and sings rock music?
One of Santa's Elvis (elves).

Who invented the light bulb and sings rock and roll?
Thomas Elvis Edison.

What early-to-rise comedian always catches the worm?

Robin Williams.

What famous Italian explorer never got dressed up?

Marco Polo Shirt.

What's brown, lumpy and wears a coonskin cap?

Gravy Crockett.

Which ugly bug was once a Wild West hero?

Buffalo Bill Cooty.

2. BIRD BRAINS

What has feathers and webbed feet?
A chicken wearing scuba gear.

How can you send a turkey through the post office?
By bird class mail.

What happened when the turkey got into a fight?
He got the stuffing knocked out of him.

Why did the turkey become the drummer in the bird band?
Because he was the one with the drumsticks.

TIM: How do you clean soot off a turkey?
SLIM: Use a feather duster.

Where is the best place to find terrified woodpeckers?

In a petrified forest.

Why was the owl so proud?

It was just listed in "Whooo's Whooo."

TEACHER: Why do baby robins leave their nests?
STUDENT: Wouldn't you leave home if your mother fed you worms?

What do you call talking birds who adopt an orphan?

Foster parrots (parents).

Show Me!

Show me a bird singing in Holland
—and I'll show you a Dutch Tweet!

Show me an owl with laryngitis
—and I'll show you a bird who doesn't give a hoot!

Show me a guy who makes jackets out of feathers . . .
and I'll show you a man who knows his way around down (town).

LON: What caramel-colored popcorn do ducks like?
RON: Quacker Jack.

What do rich ducks invest in?
  Stocks and ponds.

DENNY: What do ducks get if they eat too much
    chocolate?
JENNY: Goose pimples!

What does a goose sing at the end of its act?
  A swan song.

Knock Knock.
  Who's there?
Waddle.
  Waddle who?
Waddle I do if you don't open the door?

Inventions We Need

FEATHER TOUPEES
—for bald eagles

What would you get if you crossed a duck with a sanitation worker?
Down in the dumps.

What's the best way to ship duck eggs?
Put them in a quacker barrel.

ED: What do you have when a duck gives you smart answers?
NED: Wise quacks.

How do ducks celebrate special events?
With fire quackers.

What would you get if you crossed a tremor with a duck?
An earthquack.

15

Inventions We Need

BIRD OVERCOATS
—so they don't have to fly south

ROOSTER: When can't you borrow money from
an egg?
HEN: When the egg is broke.

What's a famous race for waterfowl?
The Kenducky Derby.

"I just got a nose job from Dr. Rooster," Mr. Duck
said to Mr. Goose.
"Oh really," Mr. Goose said. "Did it cost a lot?"
"Not much," Mr. Duck replied. "It's only a two-
dollar bill."

What did one crow telephone operator say to the
other?
"I have a caw for you."

3. IT'S A WACKY WORLD

What do you call rabbits who sky dive?
Free-falling hares.

What kind of buck carries a sample case?
A deer-to-deer salesman.

What's the best way to transport a herd of cows?
Hire a mooving van.

What do you call a scary matador?
A bull frighter.

What does a Tarzan cow swing on?
A bo-vine.

Why was the cow crying?
She was an udder failure.

What do you call an itty-bitty rodent?
Mini-mouse.

TIM: What do you give a rodent with bad breath?
SLIM: Mousewash.

TONGUE-TWISTERS

Say these 3 times quickly.

Six shy snails sighed sadly.

Pretty Patty Piggy pickles plump pink peppers.

Cheryl saw Cher's sheer shawl Sunday.

Six slick sick seals.

Sheep shouldn't sleep in shacks.

ED: What's red and white and red and white and red and white?
NED: What?
ED: Polar bear triplets with the measles.
NED: That's a really sick joke!

LARRY: What weighs a lot and bounces?
BARRY: An elephant on a pogo stick?
LARRY: Nope!
BARRY: A hippo on a trampoline?
LARRY: Nope! An overweight kangaroo.

What do you call trash carelessly thrown away by a cat?

Kitty litter.

JIM: What would you get if you crossed a rooster with morning mist?
SLIM: Cockle-Doodle-Dew!

Where do pigs like to sit?
On pork benches.

Rock and Roll 'Em in the Aisles!

What rock group do you find in an alley?
The Bowling Stones.

Where do rocks go to play golf?
Pebble Beach.

What do rocks eat for dessert?
Marble cake.

AL: Why don't rocks ever say thank you?
HAL: They take everything for granite.

Why did the silly beagle spin around in circles?
He was a top dog.

Doggie Definitions

Dog catcher—a spot remover
Pet cemetery—A doggone resting place
Bath—a magic word that makes dogs
vanish

What kind of dog is good at sniffing out young plants?

A bud hound.

RICK: What's the best way to make a dog sit?
NICK: Run him around the yard until he's too tired to stand up.

Why did Bo Peep's sheep call the police?

They'd been fleeced by a crook.

What would you get if you crossed a bagpipe with ten cents?

A fife and dime.

Claymont Schools Northside L.R.C.

What did the little chick say to the henhouse bully?
"Why don't you peck on someone your own size?"

Where does an octopus like to relax?
In an arm chair.

Why was the octopus in uniform?
He's just joined the Armed Service.

Why did the octopus take his shirt to the cleaners?
It had ink spots on it.

What did the sweaty octopus spend all of his
money on?
Underarm deodorant.

What do octopus boy scouts take camping?
Pup tent-acles.

Did You Hear About the Snowman?

—He was a really cool guy.

—He had ice water in his veins.

—He gave people the cold shoulder.

—His jokes weren't so hot.

—He quit work and started to drift.

—Finally he got into hot water and spent six months in the cooler.

Why did the snowman refuse to get married?
He got cold feet.

LARRY: Do snowmen use paste to fix things?
BARRY: No. They use igloo.

What do worm publishers print?
Underground newspapers.

23

4. WORKING FOR LAUGHS

Why was the chef in the Chinese food restaurant so tired?
He woked around the clock.

LADY: Why did I have to pay extra for the installation of this rug?
MAN: Carpet tax.

How do bees get wealthy?
They cell their honey.

SCROOGE: Where does a rich man get fresh cash?
TIM: At a money market.

Crazy Company Slogans

ACME ROPE, INC.—
>   Knot your ordinary company.

ACME MINE SHAFTS—
>   Drop in anytime.

ACME LOLLIPOPS—
>   One lick and you'll stick with us.

ACME LIGHT COMPANY—
>   We have lots of bright ideas.

ACME CLOWN MAKEUP—
>   Let us put a smile on your face.

ACME PERFUME CORP.—
>   We love it when business stinks.

ACME AIR CONDITIONING—
>   We show people how to chill out.

Why did the stupid man invest in feathers?
He heard the stock market was going down.

How's Your Job?

How's your job at the clock company?
Only time will tell.

How's your job at the banana company?
I keep slipping up.

How's your job at the travel agency?
I'm going nowhere.

How's your job on the new highway?
I'm so busy I don't know which way to turn.

How's your job at the swivel chair company?
It makes my head spin!

How's your job at the lemon juice company?
I've had bitter jobs.

GUY: Why did the baseball team hire a jeweler?
HY: They wanted to know how much their diamond was worth.

How's Your Job?

How's your job at the pie company?
It didn't pan out.

How's your job at the balloon factory?
We can't keep up with inflation.

How's your job at the crystal ball company?
I'm making a fortune.

How's your job at the history book
company?
There's no future in it.

How's your job at the clock company?
I'm having second thoughts about it.

How's your job on the farm?
Problems are cropping up.

When do four horses equal one deer?
*When the horses are quarterhorses and the deer is
a buck.*

What's the Secret of Success?

"Have concrete objectives," said the mason.

"Stay on the right track," said the race car driver.

"Make a lot of money," said the counterfeiter.

"Keep out of hot water," said the ice sculptor.

"Don't be afraid to make changes," said the babysitter.

"Keep your company growing," said the plant nursery owner.

"Stick it to the competition," said the glue manufacturer.

Man Wanted! To sell T.N.T.—Dynamite opportunity for advancement.

Why was the baby dollar crying?
It needed to be changed.

Who predicts the future and works at a bank?
The fortune teller.

What do you get if you cross a loan arranger and a gymnast?
A bank vault.

Man Wanted! To scrub floors and dust ceilings. Start at the bottom and work your way up.

Man Wanted! To work as travelling neckwear salesman. No ties.

Fired Up

What happened to the fence installer?
He was given the gate!

What happened to the carpet installer?
He got the rug pulled out from under him.

What happened to the lingerie saleslady?
She got a pink slip.

What happened to the punt returner?
He was dropped from the team.

What happened to the tuna fisherman?
He got canned!

What happened to the rock drummer?
The bandleader told him to beat it.

What happened to the plumber?
His job went down the toilet!

What happened to the lumberjack?
He was axed to leave.

How did King Kong feel when he found out he was fired?

He felt like someone had made a monkey out of him.

How did Frankenstein feel when he found out he was fired?

Shocked!

Why do mummies make good employees?

Because they get all wrapped up in their work.

How did the zombie feel when he found out he'd been fired?

He wanted to lie down and finally die.

HAL: Why did the cows go on strike?

SAL: Because they wanted moo money.

Why shouldn't you ever accept a check from a kangaroo?
Because the check will probably bounce.

JOE: Why did the miser like the male deer so much?
MOE: Because every buck was deer to him.

BOY: When I grow up I want to be an astronaut and blast way up into space.
GIRL: Talk about high hopes!

WRITER: I can't sell any of my funny short stories. What should I do?
AGENT: Try a novel approach.

Why was the watch salesman unhappy at his job?
He had too much time on his hands.

Signs of the Times

Sign in a chili powder factory—
>   WE'RE HOT STUFF!

Sign in a glove shop—
>   PLEASE GIVE US A HAND

Sign in an orange juice factory—
>   EVERYBODY CONCENTRATE!

Sign in a needle factory—
>   YOU WON'T GET STUCK WITH
>   OUR PRODUCT

Sign in a tire factory—
>   OUR WHEELS ARE ALWAYS TURNING

Sign in a calendar company—
>   ASK US FOR A DATE

Sign in a fan company—
>   OUR WORK IS A BREEZE

Sign in a clock factory—
>   WE ALWAYS HAVE TIME FOR YOU.

Sign in a pet shop—
>   BUY A DOG—GET ONE FLEA.

Silly Business Slogans

ACME TOY COMPANY—
> Our work is kids' play.

ACME PERFUME COMPANY—
> Our work is all dollars and scents.

ACME ALMOND COMPANY—
> We're nuts!

ACME SHEEP FARM—
> Our mind is on ewe.

ACME CALCULATORS—
> We help solve your problems.

ACME FLOWER BULBS—
> We root for you.

ACME PSYCHOLOGISTS—
> Visit us and you won't go away mad!

ACME POULTRY MANAGEMENT—
> Let us count your chickens before
> they hatch.

5. REALLY DUMB JOKES

Why did the dork plant pennies in his back yard?
He wanted to raise some hard cash.

What course do dweeb gardeners take in school?
Remedial weeding.

Why did the nerd go buzz buzz!
He was a bee student.

What does a dweeb study when he has a history exam the next day?
His science notes!

Dweeb Definitions

Dead ringer—a telephone that's been murdered.

Two rubber trees—a pair of stretch plants.

Principal—a teacher who has no class.

Lady wrestler—the belle of the brawl.

College—a mental institution.

Smile—a face lifter

What goes pedal! pedal! crash!?
A dork riding a bike.

RON: Where do you find fish that aren't ready for kindergarten?
JOHN: Swimming in pre-schools.

What game do baby dweebs like to play?
Geek-a-boo!

What game do little nerds like to play?
Hide and Geek.

What has leaves and is very, very, dumb?
  Dense foliage.

BEN: Why do nerds hate to eat tomato soup?
LEN: They can't get it to stay on the fork.

MERLIN: How did the silly dragon burn his fingers?
LANCELOT: When he sneezed, he covered his mouth
  with his hand. . . .

Why did the nerd bring bug spray to school?
  *His teacher told him he'd see lots of "B's" on his
  report card.*

ED: Why did the dopey boxer take up gymnastics?
NED: So he could learn to roll with the punches.

Why did the nerd wear scuba gear to the water polo game?

He wanted his coach to use him as a sub.

AL: Why did the foolish fisherman cast his line in the air instead of in the river?

HAL: He was fly fishing.

MIKE: How do you drive a clumsy car that doesn't have automatic transmission?

SPIKE: Turn on the key and step on the klutz (clutch).

How did the dork cowboy break his hand?

His boss told him to punch some cattle and that's just what he did!

Match-Maker Mirth

—They're perfectly matched. She's blinded by love and his looks are out of sight.

—They're perfectly matched. He's a history professor and she likes dates.

—They're perfectly matched. She likes to jog and he's on the run from the law!

—They're perfectly matched. She's a mermaid and there's something fishy about him.

—They're perfectly matched. She's a geologist and he has rocks in his head.

—They're perfectly matched. He's a comedian and her whole life is a joke.

—They're perfectly matched. She's a fortune teller and he has no future.

—They're perfectly matched. He's a vegetarian and she's a couch potato.

—They're perfectly matched. She's a clown and he looks funny.

Jerky Joke Jeopardy

ANSWER: Reindeer.
QUESTION: What does the weather look like, honey?

ANSWER: Annex.
QUESTION: What was Ann's full name after she married Mr. X?

ANSWER: Bewitch.
QUESTION: What insect buzzes and casts spells?

ANSWER: Blackmail.
QUESTION: What do you get when the postman spills ink in his pouch?

ANSWER: The Sahara Desert.
QUESTION: Where did the nerds go on their skiing trip?

What did the dopey barber do with his clippings?
He pasted them in a scrapbook.

6. KNOCK YOURSELF OUT

Knock Knock.
  Who's there?
Thor.
  Thor who?
Thor feet hurt!

Knock Knock.
  Who's there?
Oliver.
  Oliver who?
Oliver friends are nuts!

Knock Knock.
  Who's there?
Kerry.
  Kerry who?
Kerry me home!

Knock Knock.
  Who's there?
Ooze.
  Ooze who?
Ooze on first?

Knock Knock.
  Who's there?
Comma.
  Comma who?
Comma way with me!

Knock Knock.
  Who's there?
Empty.
  Empty who?
Empty V!

Knock Knock.
  Who's there?
All-of-her.
  All-of-her who?
All-of-her (Oliver) Stone!

Knock Knock.
  Who's there?
Robin.
  Robin who?
Robin stores is against the law!

Knock Knock.
　Who's there?
Rox N.
　Rox N. who?
Rox N. your head.

Knock Knock.
　Who's there?
Just Oodle.
　Just Oodle who?
Just Oodle you think
you are?

Knock Knock.
　Who's there?
Aunt Tillie.
　Aunt Tillie who?
Aunt Tillie (until he)
apologizes I'm staying
right here.

Knock Knock.
　Who's there?
Rolfe.
　Rolfe who?
Rolfe! Rolfe!
　Quit the barking,
　will you!

Knock Knock.
　Who's there?
Barrie.
　Barrie who?
Barrie interesting!

Knock Knock.
　Who's there?
Ivan.
　Ivan who?
Ivan looking all over
for you.

Knock Knock.
  Who's there?
Doughnut.
  Doughnut who?
Doughnut talk so loud!

Knock Knock.
  Who's there?
Dag.
  Dag who?
Dag gone! I don't know.

Knock Knock.
  Who's there?
Al B.
  Al B. Who?
Al B. home for
Christmas.

Knock Knock.
  Who's there?
Kareem.
  Kareem who?
Kareem in my coffee
makes it taste good.

Knock Knock.
  Who's there?
Wheat.
  Wheat who?
Wheat (wait) till
the sun shines, Nellie.

Knock Knock.
  Who's there?
Hugo and Al.
  Hugo and Al who?
Hugo and Al stay here.

Knock Knock.
  Who's there?
Lettuce.
  Lettuce who?
Lettuce out of here!

Knock Knock.
  Who's there?
Yale.
  Yale who?
Yale never get promoted
if you don't study.

Knock Knock.
  Who's there?
Handy.
  Handy who?
Handy test papers out.

Knock Knock.
  Who's there?
Army.
  Army who?
Army and my friends
invited to your party?

Knock Knock.
  Who's there?
Weed.
  Weed who?
Weed like a ride
on your tractor.

Knock Knock.
 Who's there?
Teller.
 Teller who?
Teller the answer.

Knock Knock.
 Who's there?
Water.
 Water who?
Water you staring at?

JAN: Knock Knock.
 DAN: Who's there?
JAN: Miss Ewe.
 DAN: Miss Ewe who?
JAN: Miss Ewe very much!

Knock Knock.
 Who's there?
Chevrolet.
 Chevrolet who?
Chevrolet an egg?

Knock Knock.
 Who's there?
Saddle.
 Saddle who?
Saddle be the day!

Knock Knock.
 Who's there?
Dotty D.
 Dotty D. Who?
Dotty D. Eyes (Dot the i's).

7. NUTTY KNOWLEDGE

Why did the teacher bring crackers to school?
For a parrot (parent)–teacher conference.

Why did the ocean marker have to stay after school?
It was a bad buoy.

MUFFY: Plus and Minus got married and guess what happened?
DUFFY: They had an addition to the family.
MUFFY: What did he turn out to be?
DUFFY: A problem child.

Sign in Clown College—

WE WANT YOU TO CLOWN AROUND IN CLASS

What did the psychologist say to the math teacher?

"I can't figure you out."

Why did the farmer go to school?

He wanted to learn how to weed better.

NEDDA: Ralph got a bad grade in drama class.

JEDDA: Yes, he acted up.

COOKING TEACHER: Sally, where is your homework?

SALLY: I don't have it, Teacher. My father ate it.

TEACHER: What are you building out of blocks?
WILLIE: A power plant.
TEACHER: Why don't you finish it?
WILLIE: I don't have enough energy.

What do you get if you cross a novel with an acrobat?
A book that can flip its own pages.

ANNE: Did you read the book about adhesive tape?
FRAN: Yes. I couldn't tear myself away from it.

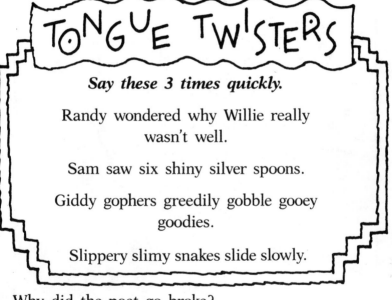

TONGUE TWISTERS

Say these 3 times quickly.

Randy wondered why Willie really wasn't well.

Sam saw six shiny silver spoons.

Giddy gophers greedily gobble gooey goodies.

Slippery slimy snakes slide slowly.

Why did the poet go broke?
Because rhyme doesn't pay.

JOE: What did you think of the novel about prison life?
MOE: The sentences were too long.

The Silly School Staff

Mrs. Greene—teacher of biology.

Mr. Mudd—teacher of earth science.

Mrs. Booker—school librarian.

Mr. Strong—gym teacher.

Mr. Sinn—vice principal.

Mr. Ford—Drivers' Ed. teacher.

Miss Step—dance teacher.

Mr. Leader—band director.

Miss Story—literature teacher.

Mrs. Payne—school nurse.

Mrs. Stern—principal

Miss Cooke—cafeteria.

Which class in school does soda like best?

Fizz Ed.

Why did the little shoelace have to stay after school?

Because it was knotty (naughty).

Knock Knock.
  Who's there?
G.I.
  G.I. who?
G.I. don't know the answer to that question!

Why did a bell ring when a monk walked into the school?
  It was time for a friar drill.

Why did Johnny bring a bowl of goldfish to class?
  Because he heard fish love to swim in schools.

Bumper Snicker—

GYM TEACHERS GIVE THEIR STUDENTS THE RUNAROUND.

TED: Did you like the photography book I sent you?

ED: I had a negative reaction.

INVENTOR: My robot dog refuses to make a sound.

BOY: Maybe he needs new bark plugs.

Inventions We Need

HORSE BLACK SUITS
—for zebras who are tired of wearing stripes.

Where does Santa like to stay when he's away from home?

At a ho-ho-hotel.

8. LET'S BUG OUT

What do you put on a baby louse when you change its diapers?

Flea powder.

LEM: Why did the bee go south for the winter?
CLEM: To visit an ant in Florida.

What do bug acrobats place under their trapeze?

A mosquito net.

What do corny spiders spin?

Cobwebs.

Don't Bee Funny

What's yellow, orange, black, and buzzes?
Carrots and bees.

Who is the happiest bug?
The glorybee.

What do you call a nosy bee?
A buzzybody.

What sport do drones play?
Beesball.

What do bees chew?
Buzzlegum.

What do you do with a chilly queen bee?
Swarm her up!

What famous bee story did Robert Louis Stevenson write?
Dr. Jekyll and Mr. Hive.

What would you get if you crossed a fast dog and a bee?
A greyhound buzz.

ED: Did you hear about the ant who went around helping people all of his life?

FRED: What happened to him?

ED: He got stepped on!

JOHN: If there are six flies on the table and you swat one of them, how many will be left?

LON: Five.

JOHN: Wrong—only one. The dead one.

What bug is very pushy?
The bold (boll) weevil.

What do ladybugs wear?
Fly (high) heel shoes.

What do you use to light up a noisy bug?
  A cricket match.

Which bug wears a toupee?
  The bald (boll) weevil.

How does an ant keep its hair in place?
  It uses bug spray.

Who are the toughest bugs at the North Pole?
  The chiller bees.

GARY: What do you get when you use expensive fly
      paper?
MARY: Stuck-up bugs.

Sign in a Beehive
MIND YOUR OWN BUZZNESS.

What do you call a male insect in Scotland?
A laddie bug.

What bug talks about you behind your back?
The cattypillar.

What kind of potatoes go oui-oui buzz-buzz?
French flies.

Insect Sports

Lice Hockey

Basketboll weevil

Gymnas-ticks

What would you get if you crossed a centipede and an elephant?
An animal that keeps tripping over its nose.

9. FUNNY FOLKS

Where did King Arthur go dancing?
  At a knight club.

When were King Arthur's soldiers too tired to fight?
  When they had too many sleepless knights.

What happened when two belly buttons had a fight?
  It was a navel battle.

What did one tea bag say to the other?
"Keep quiet or you'll get us into hot water."

Crime Time

What do baby burglars play with?
Cell blocks.

Where do baby burglars go after they're arrested?
To the state play pen.

Why don't burglars make good actors?
They try to steal the show.

What did the policeman shout to the speeding turtleneck sweater?
"Hey you, pullover!"

FRAN: What would you get if you crossed a camera with a dentist?
JAN: A picture-perfect smile?
FRAN: No. A guy with film on his teeth.

What happened to the doctor who was stuck in the chimney?
He got a flue shot.

Prescription for Fun

LADY: Doctor, doctor! My husband's mind is warped!

DOCTOR: I'll straighten him out.

LADY: Doctor, doctor, my son can't get a date!

DOCTOR: I'll fix him up.

LADY: Doctor, doctor, my father thinks he's a lightbulb!

DOCTOR: Where did he get that bright idea?

LADY: Doctor, doctor, my husband thinks he's a clock and he won't speak to anyone.

DOCTOR: He'll tock to me.

LADY: Doctor, doctor, my husband thinks he's a squirrel.

DOCTOR: Sounds like a nut case.

LADY: Doctor, doctor, my husband thinks he's a luxury car!

DOCTOR: What's so bad about that?

LADY: He gets lousy mileage.

Prescription for Fun

PATIENT: Doctor, doctor, my son thinks he's a door!

DOCTOR: Call me when he starts getting unhinged.

WIFE: Doctor, doctor, my husband thinks he's a car!

DOCTOR: Park him in the waiting room. I'll see him later.

LADY: Doctor, doctor, my husband thinks he's a car!

DOCTOR: It's probably just a gas problem.

MAN: Doctor, doctor, my brother thinks he's a rifle!

DOCTOR: Sounds like his mind is shot.

MAN: Doctor, doctor, my uncle thinks he's a trash can!

DOCTOR: I've never heard such garbage!

COACH: Doctor, doctor, one of my players thinks he's a basketball goal.

DOCTOR: Hmmm—a basket case.

How did the carpenter break all of his teeth?
He kept biting his nails.

Why did Tarzan the Ape Man join the Army
Commandos?
He wanted to learn gorilla (guerrilla) warfare.

Who was the hippest president of the U.S.?
Calvin Very Cool-idge.

Did you hear about the boy and girl vampires who
couldn't get married?
They loved in vein.

What kind of surgery does a vampire doctor
perform?
Fly-by-night operations.

Some Merry Men

What does Robin Hood wear on special occasions?
A bow tie.

Which one of Robin Hood's men carves things out of wood?
Whittle (Little) John.

Who makes the beds in Robin Hood's castle?
The upstairs Maid Marian.

What chicken was Robin Hood's friend?
Friar Cluck (Tuck).

Which member of the Merry Men is always exhausted?
Friar Tuckered Out.

What does Friar Tuck have on the front of his car?
A Robin hood ornament.

What do you call a legal expert who joins Robin Hood's band?
An outlaw-yer.

JILL: What does a barber use to write notes on?
BILL: A clipboard.

What would you get if you crossed beauticians and early-morning mist?
New hair dews (hairdos).

What would you get if you crossed a reporter with a hunting dog?
A newshound.

Why did the artist go up to the picture window?
It was time to draw the curtains.

HAL: Remember last year when I was broke? You helped me and I said I'd never forget you.
CAL: So?
HAL: Well, I'm broke again.

What would you get if you crossed a horse's path with a rainstorm?

A bridal shower.

Bumper Snickers

On an oil truck—
WE FUEL PEOPLE.

On a bookmobile—
CHECK US OUT.

On an armored car—
THIS IS A CRASH COURSE.

On a soda truck—
WE DELIVER GAS.

What ship carries lots of rabbits?

A harecraft carrier.

What would you get if you crossed a jet with a pit bull?

A plane that gets into a lot of aerial dogfights.

What do airplane pilots like to read?

Fly papers.

Why did the pilot go to the psychologist?

He thought he was plane crazy.

Loony License Plates

For a math teacher—2×2

For a student who asks a lot of
   questions—Y-NOT

For a good student—A N B

For a yodeler—U-WHO

For a bank officer—U-O-ME

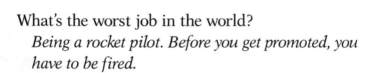

What's the worst job in the world?
Being a rocket pilot. Before you get promoted, you have to be fired.

Once during a war an army general invited an enemy general to a party. The enemy was suspicious so he didn't go, but he sent his tanks (thanks) anyway.

The Wacky Regiment

Private Matters   Major Mistake

Corporal Punishment   Colonel Korn

       General Disbelief

Uniformly Funny Stuff

What did the rubber band do when it joined the Army?
It snapped to attention.

What did the frog do when it joined the Army?
It hopped to it.

What did the waiter do when he joined the Army?
He learned how to take orders.

SARGE: Remember, soldier, your rifle is your best friend. You work together as a team.

PRIVATE: I know, Sarge, so please don't ever ask me to fire him.

What officers are in charge of military schools?
General principals.

What has antlers
and wears a uniform?
A Buck Private.

10. FUN FOOD

Where does a horse eat his morning cereal?
At the breakfast stable.

What kind of gum do oranges and lemons chew?
Juicy Fruit.

What did the orange say to the juicer?
"Give me a squeeze."

HAL: A scientist crossed an orange with an apple.
SAL: What did he get?
HAL: A perfect pair (pear).

Where's the best place to find something round and green?

Look in the limelight.

What happens when a banana gets a bad sunburn?
It starts to peel.

Why did the moron put a box of cereal out in the freezing cold?

He wanted Frosted Flakes.

BETTY: What would you get if you crossed a breakfast cereal and a stunt plane?
EDDIE: Fruit Loop-the-Loops!

What kind of coffee do squirrels drink in the morning?

Chuck-Full-of-Nuts.

What has a yolk and plays heavenly music?
A harp-boiled egg.

Why do lions always eat lunch?
It's their mane meal!

How do you fix a broken pizza?
Use tomato paste.

What would you get if you crossed chili peppers with frankfurters?

Hot, hot, hot, hotdogs.

What would you get if you crossed a hamburger stand with a novel?

A fast food store-y.

What do sharks eat at barbecues?

Clamburgers.

Why was the shark's throat so dry?

He ate a peanut butter and jellyfish sandwich.

What kind of sandwiches do whales eat for lunch?

Peanut blubber sandwiches.

What sandwich is chewy and honks a lot?

A peanut butter and traffic jam sandwich.

What do skunks like to eat for lunch?

Peanut butter and smelly sandwiches.

AL: Where's the best place to be if you're sandwich
    meat?
CAL: Home in bread.

What kind of soup do goats like to have for lunch?
Alpha-butt soup.

Inventions We Need

EXTRA-SMALL ROLLER SKATES
—for snails who want to travel faster

MARGARINE: How old are you?
TOAST: Old enough to know butter (better).

Why did the suspect go into the kitchen?
To cook up an alibi.

LENA: Let's snack on fruit and watch a horror movie.
GINA: Why should we do that?
LENA: Because I want to eat peaches and scream.

GINA: What kind of vegetable should we have tonight?

TINA: Beets me.

Sign on a Vegetable Stand—

ALWAYS SAY PEAS.

Why was the cornstalk crying?
It had an earache.

What vegetable has trouble breathing?
Asparagasp!

What kind of band did the Chinese cooks form?
A wok and roll band.

DELLA: Are you making mud pies?
STELLA: No. A meatloaf.
DELLA: How can you make a meatloaf out of dirt?
STELLA: I use ground round.

SANDY: What is that book doing in the frying pan?
MANDY: It says "cookbook," so I did.

Bumper Snicker—

**On a neighborhood snack food truck—
WE'RE CHIPS ON THE
OLD BLOCK**

What did one potato chip send to the other in
December?
   A Crispness card.

NED: What is the main ingredient in Lassie's dog
     biscuits?
JED: Collie flour.

MAN: How are your grape plants?
FARMER: They're vine, thanks.

Why did the dieter throw a dish of ice cream across
the pond?
   He wanted to skip dessert.

Attention!

The Green Giant has corns!

What has a rubber heel, two wings, and is sweet?
Shoe-fly pie.

What are round, chewy, and have horns?
Goatmeal cookies.

Bumper Snicker

On a bakery truck—
DOUGHNUT PASS US BY

What do space squirrels like to eat?
Astronuts.

11. SPORT SNICKERS

What game do cards play while on ships?
Shuffleboard.

What game does playground equipment play?
Slide and seek.

What game did the two mountains play?
Valleyball.

What coughs and fires bullets?
A sick shooter.

What does a rabbit pilot fly?
A hare plane.

Why did the tennis fan get his eyes examined?
Because he was seeing doubles.

What do you get if you cross an Olympic champion with a pair of sneakers?
Very athletic shoes.

Did you hear about the monster who went to the gym? It didn't work out.

What would you get if you crossed a camera with a body builder?
Film that develops itself at the gym.

What do prize fighters wear under their clothes?
Boxer shorts.

Why did the really dumb boxer come to the prize fight in a bathing suit?

Because his manager told him he was going to take a dive.

Why did the man with amnesia take up running?

He wanted to jog his memory.

Sign in a Dance Studio—

WATCH YOUR STEP.

What was the matter with the sick jogger?

He kept running a temperature.

MACK: What kind of shirts do golfers wear?

JACK: Tee shirts.

What do you get if you cross an antique with a golfer?

Someone definitely old enough to drive.

Where did the horse play table tennis?

On a Ping-Pong stable.

What kind of basketball nets do they use in Hawaii?

Hula hoops.

What's the best thing to do when a soccer ball is in the air?

Use your head.

And Then Some!

—And then there was the sly basketball player who always got the jump on the competition.

—And then there was the dentist who joined the Army so he could become a drill sergeant.

—And then there was the frankfurter who was a born wiener (winner).

—And then there was the millionaire boxer who only fought in diamond rings.

—And then there was the wrestler who could never get a hold of his friends.

What's crisp, salty, and floats?
Potato ships.

How does a monster football player score a touchdown?
He runs over the ghoul line.

Who delivers mail to football players?
The goal post man.

What does an owl cheerleader say?
"Whoo-ray! Whoo-ray!"

Why did the plant become a cheerleader?
So it could root for the home team.

What is Transylvania's national sport?
Drac racing.

What does a miser wear when he goes to the ice rink?
Cheap skates.

Why did the track and field star yell in pain?
He slipped his discus.

TIM: Why doesn't Tarzan like to play games with his pet?

JIM: Because his pet is a cheetah.

What throws fastballs and is made of glass?
A pitcher (picture) window.

What do you bring onto a baseball field if a player gets injured in the seventh inning?
The Seventh Inning Stretch-er.

What is a burglar's favorite place in baseball?
Safe at home!

What runs around a track and goes "Choo! choo!"
A jogger with hayfever.

Knock Knock.
Who's there?
Randy.
Randy who?
Randy marathon but I lost.

ZACK: What do trees do before a marathon?
JACK: Root for each other?
ZACK: No. They limb-er up.

What animal lives at the North Pole and scores strikes and spares?
A bowler (polar) bear.

What did the bowling pins say to the bowling ball?
"Please spare us."

12. LAUGHS GALORE!

Why didn't the rhino pass inspection?
  His horn didn't work.

Why wouldn't the ewe kiss the ram?
  He had baa breath.

What's ten feet tall, hairy, and limps?
  A Sasquatch with a sprained ankle.

What would you get if you crossed a lion with fast-moving water?
  A roaring river.

TV Time

What TV news reporter sinks to the bottom of the ocean?
The anchorman.

What is a foot doctor's favorite TV game show?
Heel of Fortune.

Why did the big game hunter go to Hollywood?
He wanted to shoot a movie.

What shows rock videos and melts in your mouth, not in your hand?
M & MTV.

When does a baby TV cry?
When its channel needs changing.

Why was there a cast on the TV set?
It just had a station break.

What kind of TV show is relaxing to watch?
A sit calm.

Crazy Calls

Why was the telephone shaking?
It just had a close call.

What is a crow's favorite phone service?
Caw waiting (call waiting).

What phone service do lumberjacks use?
Tree-way calling (three-way calling).

What would you get if you crossed corn
with a telephone?
Golden earrings.

Why did the telephone go to a psychologist?
It had too many hangups.

What kind of card do you send to a sick stream?
A get-well creek (quick) card.

Sign in a Magic Shop—
WE KNOW EVERY TRICK IN THE BOOK.

Did you hear about the magician who really loved
rabbit tricks? He joined the Hare Club for Men.

What would you get if you crossed a garbage dump with a post office?

Junk mail.

What would you get if you crossed a magician with an alarm clock?

A magic tick.

What would you get if you crossed homing pigeons with Christmas presents?

Gifts that return themselves to the store if you don't like them.

MATT: What did the ghost buy for his haunted house?
PAT: Home Moaner's (Owner's) Insurance.

Why did everyone call the whale a bully?

Because he liked to pick on shrimps.

Idiotic Inventions

A refrigerated stove
—for cooking cold suppers.

Toupees made out of grass
—for bald spots in the lawn.

Eatable sandwich bags
—so you don't have to unwrap your lunch.

Boomerang litter
—so trash returns to the person who threw it away.

Hinky Pinky

What do you call a dumb gobbler?
A jerky turkey.

What do you call a gobbler who thinks he knows everything?
A smirky turkey.

What do you call a dweeb piggy?
A dorky porky.

What do you call a bee with asthma?
A beezer wheezer.

What do you call a small bug's trousers?
Ant's pants.

What do you call a slightly overweight chimp?
A chunky monkey.

What do you call a friendly dead Egyptian?
A chummy mummy.

Why was the piano laughing?
Someone kept tickling its keys.

What did the clock say to the wristwatch?
"I enjoyed tocking with you, but now you're starting to tick me off."

How do you make a clock cry?
Twist its arms.

Why did Mrs. Clock wash her kids?
Because they had dirty faces.

What would you get if you crossed a flock of sheep and an Ice Age elephant?
A very woolly mammoth.

Which dinosaur could cast magic spells?
Tyrannosaurus Hex.

Where is the best place to keep pigs in a house?
   In a swine cellar.

Why did the boat go on a diet?
   Because it wasn't ship-shape.

How did the sailor break his bathroom scale?
   He tried to weigh his ship's anchor.

What would you get if you crossed a small ocean
marker with a ghost?
   Little Buoy Boo.

What princess cried a lot because a witch cast a
spell on her?
   Weeping Beauty.

Who Said That?

Said the topsoil—"I hate it when people
treat me like dirt."

Said the broken ruler—"I just don't
measure up."

Said the rubber band—"I've got to snap out
of it!"

Said the paper—"I've gone completely
blank!"

Tall Tales

Once there was a princess who got everything backwards. Every prince she kissed turned into a toad.

There's a jungle so tough that bananas grow in gangs instead of bunches.

There's a desert so dry, camels won't cross it without carrying a canteen.

How does a rabbit keep cool in summer?
He installs central hare conditioning.

What would you get if you crossed a rabbit with a mad doctor?
Hare-brained experiments.

What would you get if you crossed a photographer with a geometry teacher?
Weird camera angles.

MAN: Don't slam the door like that!
LADY: I'm sorry. Is the door that expensive?
MAN: Of course it is. Solid oak doesn't grow on trees, you know.

Where does a mermaid sleep?
On a water bed.

What do you call a big goat who picks on little kids?
A bully (billy) goat.

What do you call a silly goat?
A ninny (nanny) goat.

What did the hen tell the immature rooster?
"Why don't you crow up?"

What would you get if you crossed a chicken with a bicycle?
A hen-speed bike.

When is a sick horse well enough to have visitors?
When he's in stable condition.

Why did the lady horse put on a wedding dress?
She was headed down the bridal (bridle) path.

What did the angry horse say to the rider who nagged him?
"Get off my back!"

Sign on a Horse Stable—

WE NEVER STAND BEHIND OUR PRODUCT

Wedding Blisters

—If Miss Piggy married Mr. Back
   . . . she'd be Piggy Back.

—If Clara Barton married Mr. Nett
   . . . she'd be Clara Nett.

—If Shirley Temple married Mr. Ujest
   . . . she'd be Shirley Ujest (Surely you jest).

—If Snow White married Mr. Fall
   . . . she'd be Snow Fall.

—If Olive Oyl married Mr. Pitts
   . . . she'd be Olive Pitts.

What did the wall say to the bookcase?
   "Help yourshelf."

What did one doorknob say to the other?
   "It's your turn."

What did the absent-minded idiot say to his identical twin?
   "Gee, you look familiar."

INDEX